SMART BRAIN RIGHT BRAIN

Let's Build

Om Kidz | Om Books International

Reprinted in 2023

Corporate & Editorial Office
A-12, Sector 64, Noida 201 301
Uttar Pradesh, India
Phone: +91 120 477 4100
Email: editorial@ombooks.com
Website: www.ombooksinternational.com

Sales Office
107, Ansari Road, Darya Ganj
New Delhi 110 002, India
Phone: +91 11 4000 9000
Email: sales@ombooks.com

Author: Shweta Sinha
Editor: Kirti Pathak
Art & Design: Anshuman Pandey, Gaurav Bhandari, Harish Arya

ISBN: 978-93-52768-42-4

Printed in India

10 9 8 7 6 5 4 3 2

CONTENTS

1. A History of Houses

The early man lived in caves. Caves provided shelter and protection from the weather and wild animals.

A cave is a natural hollow space in the ground that is large enough for a human to enter.

During the Ice Age, humans learnt to build tents using mammoth skin and bones.

POCKET FACT

People in different parts of the world use different materials to build houses depending on what is available in their area.

People started making sun-dried bricks as early as 4,000 BC. Soon, they learnt that baking bricks in an oven made them stronger.

Most houses in ancient Egypt were built with sun-dried bricks made with clay taken from the river Nile.

During the middle ages, huts made of stone with thatched roofs were common in Europe.

Rich people lived in stone castles.

Modern cities have buildings of all sizes. Most buildings are made of bricks. Some are made of wood.

DID YOU KNOW?

The Inuit people of the Arctic live in igloos. An igloo is a house made of ice. The ice keeps the inside warm.

2. How to Build a House

Many people are involved in constructing a house.

First, an architect draws up a plan for the house. A floor plan tells us how big each room will be in the house.

The architect then brings on board a team of different professionals to help in the task of building the house.

The general contractor makes sure that everyone on the team works according to the plan.

POCKET FACT

An architect is a person who designs buildings. Architects make drawings with pens, pencils, and even computers.

The first crew at the building site prepares the site and builds the foundation of the house. The foundation supports the weight of the house. A strong foundation keeps the house strong.

Bulldozers are used to clear the site of any trees, rocks and debris. The ground is levelled. Heavy equipments are used to dig up holes and trenches in the ground. Concrete is poured into the holes and trenches. This forms the foundation of the house.

Pouring concrete to build the foundation

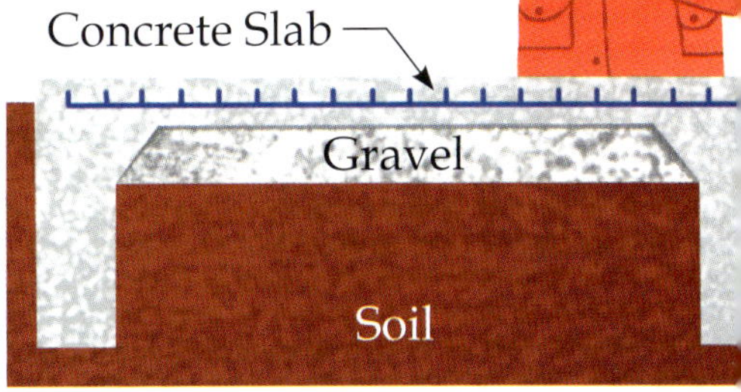

Cross-section of a Foundation

DID YOU KNOW?

Many different types of tools, machinery and heavy equipments are used to construct a house.

Building the framework

Once the foundation is ready, the framing crew takes over. They start by laying down the floor. The walls are then assembled on the floor according to the design. Space for doors and windows are left open in the walls. Roof framing is done.

Inside, the house begins to look enclosed. Doors and windows arrive and are fixed in their spaces. The roof and walls are covered with waterproof material.

POCKET FACT

The indigenous people of North America lived in tents called **Tepees.** The walls of a tepee are made of animal skin and wooden poles.

Interiors

Now the interior work begins. The plumbers install the water pipes and the sewage system. The electricians run the wires through the walls and fix the sockets and switches. They set up the main fuse box to keep the house safe from any power overloading.

The walls and ceiling are insulated to lower heating and cooling costs. The drywall is put up. It covers all the cracks and nails in the interior walls.

Carpenters build cabinets and other woodwork in the house.

DID YOU KNOW?

Landscape artists keep working on growing plants and grass around the house while the construction is going on.

Once the cabinets are in, the interior doors are installed. It is time to paint the walls and put up the wallpapers. The floors are carpeted and tiled. The house is now ready to move in and be called a **Home**!

3. Magnificent Monuments

Over the years, people have built some remarkable structures all over the world.

The La Sagrada Família (Barcelona, Spain)

Antoni Gaudí started building this church in 1882. The design of the church was inspired by many forms of nature. Its interior pillars resemble trees. The two-storey high stained glass windows throw colourful light patterns on the white walls.

The Leaning Tower (Pisa, Italy)

This is a bell tower that tilts to one side. The tower was not designed to lean. But its foundation on soft subsoil caused one side to sink in the ground during its construction. It is a miracle that the tower hasn't yet crashed to the ground.

The Taj Mahal (Agra, India)

An emperor built this stunning tomb for his wife in the 17th century. Made of white marble, the onion-domed building glows like snow on moonlit nights.

DID YOU KNOW?

La Sagrada Família has been under construction for over a century and is expected to be completed by 2026.

4. Gems of the Ancient World

The Great Pyramid

The Great Pyramid is the only surviving member of the seven wonders of the ancient world. It was built as a tomb for an ancient king.

The Great Pyramid is the largest single building in the world. It took decades and thousands of workers to construct it. This huge building is made up of two million stone blocks. Some stone blocks weigh more than four elephants!

The Sphinx is a strange looking stone sculpture next to the Great Pyramid. It has a lion's body and a king's head. It guards the king's tomb.

POCKET FACT

Location: Giza, Egypt
Materials: Limestone

The base of the pyramid is bigger than five football grounds.

The Great Wall of China

This is the world's longest wall running for about 21,196 km . It was constructed as a defense against enemy attacks. The first Chinese Emperor, Qin Shai Hong started building the wall, but not much of this first wall remains. The current wall was built by the Ming dynasty.

The wall took over 2,000 years to complete. Millions of people worked in the construction.

The Great Wall is not a continuous wall but is made up of a number of different sections.

POCKET FACT

Location: China
Materials: Compacted earth, stone and brick

The Colosseum

This stadium was once the most popular location in Rome. Built by Emperor Vespasian of the Flavian dynasty, it was the largest of all Roman amphitheatres. The stadium was used as a games arena to stage bloody combats between armed fighters, known as gladiators.

This three-storey building took nine years to build. 40,000 to 50,000 spectators could sit inside the stadium

Over the centuries, the Colosseum has withstood serious damages by fire, earthquakes and vandals.

The Colosseum is oval-shaped, similar to several modern sports arenas.

A maze of tunnels underneath the structure was used to hold slaves and animals, which were to be used in a contest. The tunnels connected different parts of the arena to each other.

POCKET FACT

Location: Rome, Italy
Materials: Stone

5. Marvels from the Middle Ages

The Notre Dame Cathedral

On a small island in the middle of the River Seine stands one of the most famous landmarks of France. It is the 800-year-old Notre Dame Cathedral.

The cathedral is built in the French Gothic style. Gothic cathedrals have spires and flying buttresses to strengthen their large walls.

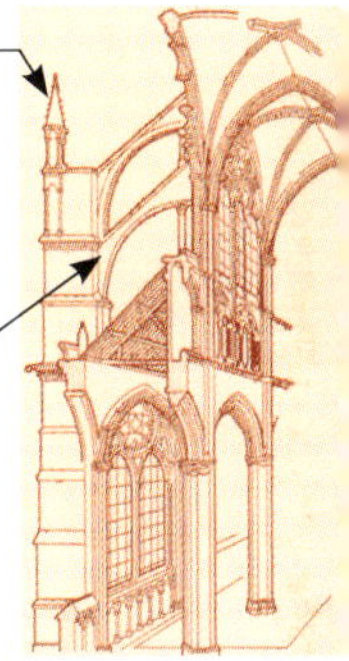

The three round-shaped (rose) windows on the cathedral are the biggest in Europe.

On 15 April 2019 a massive fire broke out in the cathedral. It burnt for over half a day and caused massive damage to the building.

POCKET FACT

Location: Paris, France
Materials: Stone and brick

The Blue Mosque

The dazzling Sultan Ahmed mosque is also called the Blue Mosque because of the blue tiles on its interior walls. It was built by the Ottoman ruler, Sultan Ahmed I. The monument is still an active mosque, where prayers are offered five times a day.

The huge central dome is supported by four thick pillars called elephant legs.

Tall, narrow minarets are a prominent feature.

260 stained glass windows keep the interiors well-lit by filtering in natural light.

The Blue Mosque faces the Hagia Sofia, another famous mosque in Istanbul. Hagia Sofia was an ancient church which was later converted into a mosque by adding minarets.

POCKET FACT

Location: Istanbul, Turkey
Materials: Stone and marble

The Kailash Temple

Imagine constructing the roof of a house first and then building the walls. Do you think this can be done?

This astonishing temple has not been built up like other buildings. It has been built top to bottom by carving downwards into a hill. No other structure in the world has been made this way.

200,000 tonnes of rock had to be removed by hand before the carving for the temple could even begin.

The entire temple complex is made of a single rock chiselled by hand.

The structure was designed to resemble Mount Kailash, believed to be the abode of Lord Shiva, the presiding deity of the temple.

POCKET FACT

Location: Ellora, India
Materials: Volcanic rock

6. Modern Structures

The Sydney Opera House

The Sydney Opera House is the busiest performing arts centre in the world. It is perched on a tongue of land jutting out into the Sydney Harbour.

The Opera Theatre is used for performances of opera, ballet and dance.

The Opera house is a complex of 1,000 rooms - theatres and halls - linked unerneath the huge shell-like roofs.

Over 2,500 people can sit together and watch a performance in the main concert hall. Over two million people visit the opera house every year.

The Guggenheim Museum

In the Upper East Side of Manhattan sits a unique circular building that stands out among the tall skyscrapers. The building is a museum to display famous paintings. This museum is named after its founder, Solomon R. Guggenheim.

A limestone building with flat walls was later added to the complex. Flat walls were easier for fixing paintings than the curved walls of the original building.

The building is wider at the top than at the bottom. Some people think it looks like a spaceship.

Inside, a continuous ramp spirals around an atrium. The white walls along the ramp show off the vibrant artwork. Visitors climb to the top of the building on an elevator, then walk down the ramp, enjoying the displays. A giant glass dome floods the building with light.

POCKET FACT

Location: New York, USA
Materials: Reinforced concrete, limestone

7. Spectacular Skyscrapers

Extremely tall buildings are known as skyscrapers. Skyscrapers are almost always found in big cities. There is little space in our crowded cities to build sideways. So, architects now build slender, tall buildings that seem to reach up to the clouds.

The first modern skyscraper was built in 1885. It was the Home Insurance Building in Chicago. The building was only 10 storeys tall. Some of the tallest buildings today have more than 100 storeys!

Here are some of the tallest buildings in the world.

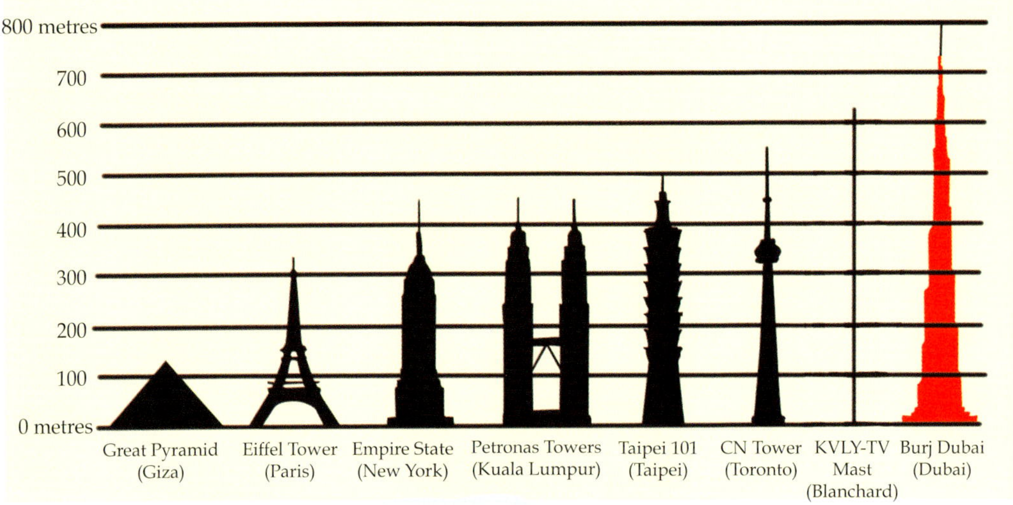

DID YOU KNOW?

Originally, the word skyscraper was a term used for the triangular sails on a ship.

Why don't skyscrapers topple down?

Have you tried building a tall tower with Lego blocks? If you keep stacking blocks on top of each other, the tower becomes unstable. It may even fall down and break. So how do tall buildings remain standing?

- It is normal for skyscrapers to sway a little in the wind. But too much swaying can topple it over. To avoid swaying too much, builders strengthen the concrete used in construction with steel rods and beams.

- Buildings need a strong foundation to stay stable. The part of the building under the ground is called the substructure or foundation. To build a sturdy base, workers dig deep down and even blast into the solid rock deep below the layer of soil.

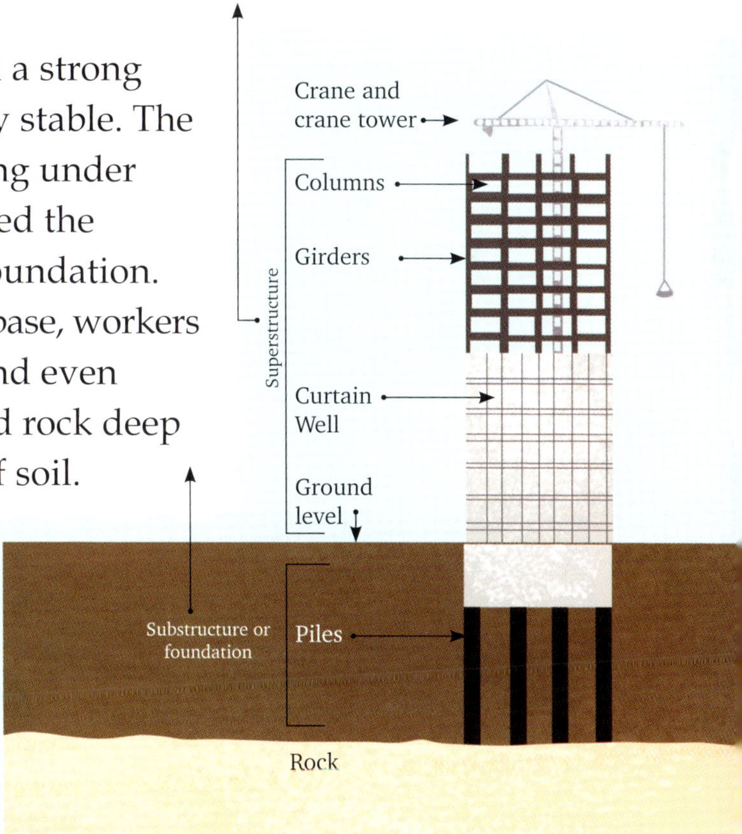

The Burj Khalifa

The Burj Khalifa soars high above everything around it. Infact if you could line up all the tall buildings of the world, Burj Khalifa would soar above all of them.

The Burj Khalifa is the tallest building in the world.

The weight of the concrete used to build the Burj equals 100,000 elephants.

POCKET FACT

How high: 163 storeys (828 m)
Location: Dubai
Function: Mixed use with residential apartment, hotel and office

The Shanghai Tower

This is the second tallest building in the world after Burj Khalifa. It is the tallest in China.

The Shanghai Tower has a unique twisted design. It has the fastest elevators in the world. You can climb to the world's highest observation deck on the 121st floor for an amazing view of the Huangpu River. The building also houses one of the highest hotels in the world. This huge tower took seven years to build and was completed in 2015.

POCKET FACT

How high: 128 storeys (632 m)
Location: Shanghai, China
Function: Hotel, office and retail shop

The Flame Towers

If you visit Baku, the capital city of Azerbaijan, you will come across buildings that seem to be on fire. Don't panic! These three supercool skyscrapers are merely designed to look like flames. Azerbaijan is also known as the 'land of fire'. This incredible flame architecture pays homage to the country's nickname.

LED screens completely cover the buildings on the outside. The screens flicker and flare, displaying the movement of fire. This makes it appear as if the towers are burning.

POCKET FACT

How high: The tallest of the trio has 39 storeys (182 m)
Location: Baku, Azerbaijan
Function: Each Flame Tower has a separate use: residential, hotel and office

The Eiffel Tower

This iconic landmark used to be the tallest manmade structure in the world until 1930. The Eiffel Tower is named after Gustave Eiffel, a civil engineer who designed the structure. Gustave Eiffel has also designed some parts of the Statue of Liberty in New York.

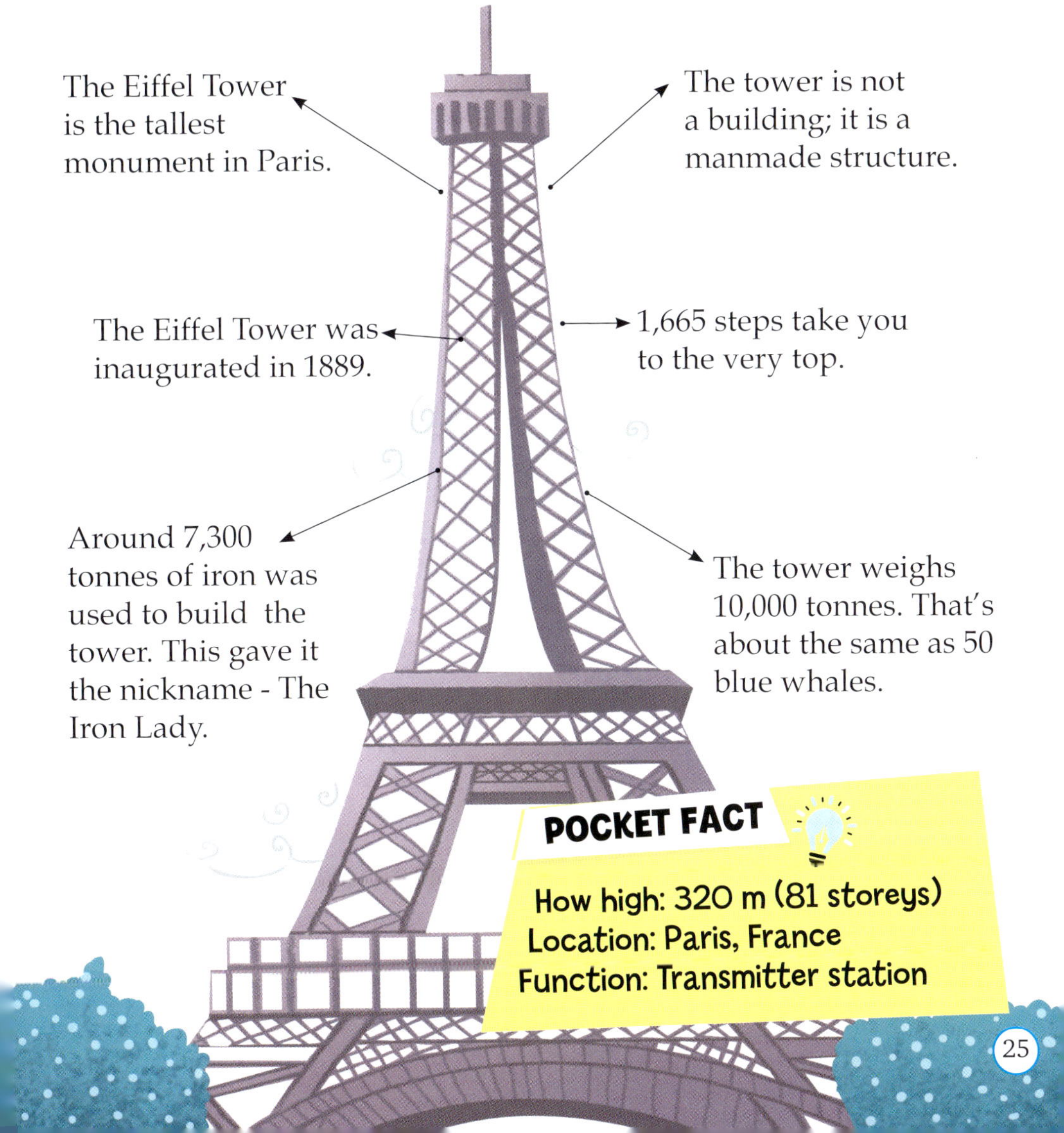

POCKET FACT

How high: 320 m (81 storeys)
Location: Paris, France
Function: Transmitter station

8. Activity: Let's Make a Skyscraper

You can also build your own miniature city with waste materials, toys and a little bit of imagination.

You need:

- Empty toilet rolls. You can use as many as you want.
- Paints and paintbrushes.
- Scissors.

Step 1: Cut out four slits at both ends of the paper rolls.

Step 2: Paint the toilet rolls in different colours. Then make windows with paint.

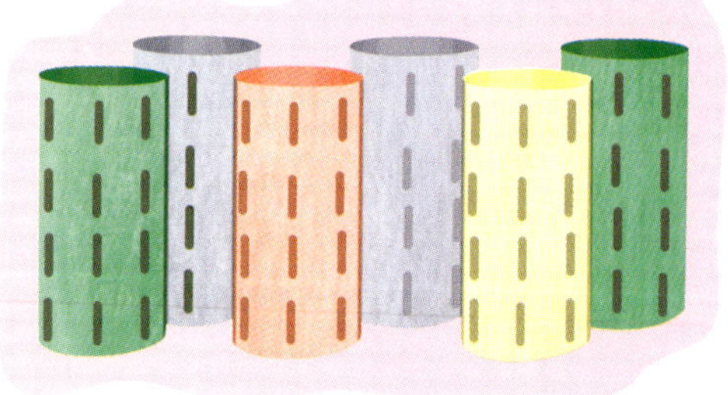

Step 3: Stack the rolls using the slits you made in the rolls. Use your imagination to stack them anyway you like.

Step 4: Bring out your miniature toys and line them up around your buildings to create a whole city. You can even use black card paper around the buildings for roads.

Tip: Make buildings of different sizes in the same manner using kitchen paper tubes or empty cereal boxes.

POCKET FACT

Until 1970, the Empire State building, New York, remained the tallest skyscraper in the world. It has 73 elevators and you can reach the 80th floor from the first floor in just a minute.

Match the following

Match the picture of the building to the correct name.

1. 	(a) Burj Khalifa
2. 	(b) Colosseum
3. 	(c) Sultan Ahmed mosque
4. 	(d) Great Wall of China
5. 	(e) Eiffel Tower

True or False

Joan and Alice had been on a trip around the world with their parents. They visited many famous buildings. Help them find out the correct facts about the buildings.

1. The Leaning Tower of Pisa was designed to tilt.
   (True/False)
2. Joan was amazed to see the dazzling white dome of the Taj Mahal.
   (True/False)
3. The Kailash Temple is built of a single stone.
   (True/False)
4. Alice watched a movie at the Sidney Opera House.
   (True/False)
5. The Eiffel Tower was built using tonnes of concrete.
   (True/False)
6. Joan and Alice saw a strange statue with a lion's body and a man's head near the Giant Pyramids.
   (True/False)

Choose the Correct Answer:

1. Which is the tallest building in the world?

   (a) Empire State Building (b) Shanghai Towers

   (c) Burj Khalifa

2. This building is the only surviving member of the Seven Wonders of the Ancient World.

   (a) The Taj Mahal (b) The Great Pyramids

   (c) The Great Wall of China

3. The Inuit people of the Arctic live in ________.

   (a) Igloos (b) Tepees

   (c) Castles

4. Ancient Egyptian houses were built with sun-dried bricks made with clay taken from which river?

   (a) Huangpu (b) Nile

   (c) Seine

5. The Guggenheim Museum was built to display ______.

   (a) Scientific discoveries

   (b) Archaeological artefacts

   (c) Famous paintings

6. The Eiffel Tower is a famous landmark in which city?

   (a) London (b) Paris

   (c) New York

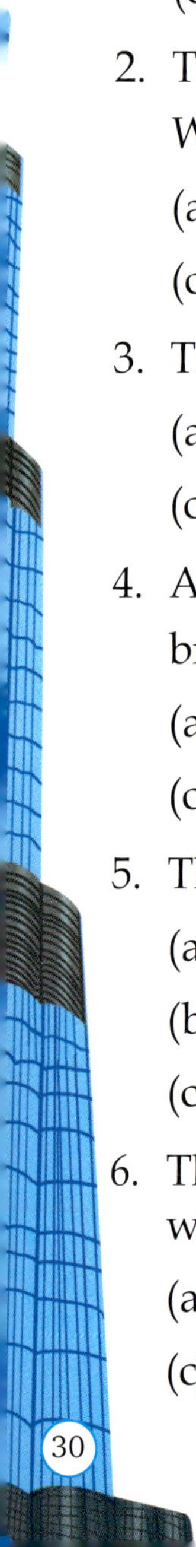

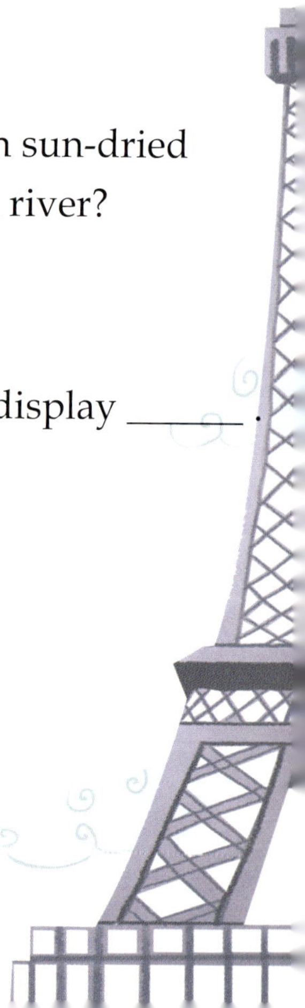

Jumbled Words

Unscramble the jumbled word to find out the correct answer.

1. Really tall buildings are called ___________ .
   (RRSSKAEPYC)
2. An ____________ is a person who designs buildings.
   (AIETTCCRH)
3. The __________ is the first thing to be built when building a house. (FNOOUINTDA)
4. An ____________ sets up the fuse box to keep the house safe from any power overloading. (RTICCIANEEL)
5. The ______________ was a games arena to stage bloody combats between gladiators. (MSSOOUELC)
6. The _______ ______cathedral is built in the French Gothic style. (ENORT MEAD)

GLOSSARY

Amphitheatre	an open circular or oval building with a central space surrounded by tiers of seats for spectators
Ancient	belonging to the very distant past and no longer in existence
Arena	a level area surrounded by seating, in which sports, entertainments, and other public events are held
Atrium	a central hall in a modern building
Beam	a long, sturdy piece of squared timber or metal used to support the roof or floor of a building
Combat	fighting between armed forces
Compacted	firmly packed or pressed together
Concrete	a building material made from a mixture of broken stone or gravel, sand, cement, and water
Construction	the action of building something
Deity	a god or goddess
Pre-historic	very old or out of date
Vandal	a person who deliberately destroys or damages property belonging to others

ANSWERS

Page 28. 1. (b) 2. (d) 3. (a)
4. (e) 5. (c)

Page 29. 1. False 2. True 3. True
4. False 5. False 6. True

Page 30. 1. (c) 2.(b) 3. (a)
4. (b) 5. (c) 6. (b)

Page 31. 1. Skyscrapers 2. Architect
3. Foundation 4. Electrician
5. Colosseum 6. Notre Dame